CONVERSATIONS WITH GOD

The Devotional

Cherie Barnes

Relentless Publishing House, LLC

Columbia, SC

RELENTLESS
PUBLISHING

Coversations With God : The Devotional
Copyright © 2018 by Cherie Barnes.

Published By :
Relentless Publishing House, LLC
www.relentlesspublishing.com

RELENTLESS
PUBLISHING

ISBN: 9781948829373

Second Edition: November 2019

10 9 8 7 6 5 4 3 2 1

Dedication

To Nia:
May you always look to the Lord for
comfort

TABLE OF CONTENTS

INTRODUCTION

The eternal God is your refuge, and underneath are the everlasting arms

Deuteronomy 33:27 NIV

C onversations with God: The Devotional is filled with different losses that we experience and/or might suffer in life. The "Conversations" are in part some of the things that I have shared in my prayer time with God. Other experiences are from ones I have been privileged to be a part of. There is no exact time or period when one will get over losing a loved one or recover from an experience. As I discussed in my first book, "12 Lessons of Healing Through Grief", it takes time. Recalling the memories of what you had with your loved one is what you have to look forward to in order to be comforted. Remembering the experiences, you have gathered with each loss teaches patience, steadfastness, and humility. It is a journey and will take some time. Some losses are harder to get over such as the loss of a child or of a parent. Read these devotionals, share them with others and know that God is infinite and that his wisdom is always there to comfort you.

LOSS OF A PARENT

He will wipe away every tear from their eyes and death shall be no more, neither shall there be mourning, nor crying, nor pain anymore, for the former things have passed away.

Revelation 21:4

It is hard to experience the loss of anyone in our lives, but the hardest thing in the world is to lose a parent. When I was growing up I said that my parents would live forever. In God's wisdom, he saw fit to award my father his heavenly wings when I was 16 years old. Being so young I did not understand why and now after 25 + years, I still do not know. As I am growing in my Christian walk, I know that God is powerful and has wisdom is forever more. I am learning to remember love, the memories and all the in between. When a parent passes away it hurts deeply; and that you never get over it, we just learn to deal with it. I often wonder how my life would be if my father was still here. I will ponder this forever more and remember the good times as "Daddy's Little Girl".

Prayer

Lord help me to remember that you are Omnipotent and that my memories are always there to help me, even when I'm down. Heavenly Father, I need you to hold my hand and walk alongside me, help me make the best decisions and allow me to draw strength from you. Amen.

LOSS OF A PET

Are not five sparrows sold for two pennies? Yet not one of them is forgotten by God.

Luke 12:6

Experiencing the loss of a pet can have a great impact on a pet parent and family members. Most pets are considered part of a family and their loss can bring up feelings of grief and mourning. Having a pet makes a person responsible, teaches them patience and prepares them if they are choosing to be a parent. Sometimes people do not get over the loss of a pet due to the fact that the pet was a part of the family. Do not dwell on the loss, but choose to embrace and remember it. If God takes care of the animals and even the birds, he will heal the heart of a pet parent.

Prayer
Thank you for the love that I received from my pet. Although he is not here to sit with me, let me remember him fondly and all the love that I received. Amen.

LOSS OF EMPLOYMENT

I will instruct you and teach you concerning the path you should walk; I will direct you with my eye

Psalm 32:8

How could this happen to me! I did everything that I know how to do. I got to work on time and sometimes early. I worked through my lunch most days, I volunteered for special projects and I still lost my job. How could this possibly happen to me? I can only imagine that there is something much better in store for me. I've wanted to start my own business, but maybe I can't do it and devote the time needed because I am working a full-time job. Only you God know what's best for me. Thank you for developing my humility, patience, and trust during this process.

Prayer

Heavenly Father thank you for bringing a new start to my life, I trust you and know that you are not a liar. You have other plans for me that I just do not see. Thank you for the abundance of blessing that you will now fulfill. In Jesus name, Amen.

LOSS OF FINANCES

And my God will supply every need of yours according to his riches in glory in Christ Jesus.

Philippians 4:19

We have seen the documentaries on television about ordinary people who win sweepstakes or lottery pools only to find that they are broke a few short years later. Our society is one that is materialistic and we have to have the things right away. We sometimes do not have that patience in order to make sure that our finances are ok with a windfall of that kind. We make bad decisions and this leads to a loss of finances. Not only with the lottery and sweepstakes but by living above our means, by over abusing credit cards, mismanaging our available funds, losing a job, being laid off of a job or a temporary loss of employment can all lead to a loss of finances. We may do a number of other things leading to the loss of finances, but knowing that God will supply our needs is comforting even when we do not see it.

Prayer

Father, help us to be a better steward of our finances. Allow us to understand what we are doing with our money and give us the guidance and resources to do better and to make the best choices we can. Amen.

LOSS OF A SPOUSE

The Lord is my portion, says my soul,
Therefore I hope in him.

Lamentations 3:24

When a person loses a spouse this can be for a few reasons. It can be because of death, sickness, divorce or separation. This impacts the whole family and makes it difficult for the family to move forward. The loss of a spouse can lead to an impact in finances, housing and security. If there are children involved this affects them as well and a plan should be put in place in order to support the loss. God will provide and send people to you In order to help you and to be your support system. He will take you from being fearful to being confidents to being able to utilize what he has chosen for you to help you get through.

Prayer

Father help me to know that losing my spouse was in your will. I surrender all to you even though I do not understand. I know that you have destined a time and place for everything in our lives. Help me to continue to press on. Amen.

LOSS OF A CHILD(REN)

Lo, Children are an heritage of the Lord; and the fruit of the womb is his reward.

Psalm 127:3

There is a saying that a parent should never experience the loss of a child. It seems in this day and age that, this is happening more and more often due to gun violence, accidental deaths, drugs addiction and even incarceration. All of these things can lead to losing a child(ren). It is never easy losing a child but there are certain things that are lost if this happens. The loss of security, the loss of a mothers touch, the loss of a listening ear and even the loss of not being able to touch your child is what happens when one loses that child.

Prayer
God bring comfort and peace to me as I remember my child. Your name means peace, so I ask that you help me experience it on today. In your precious name, I pray, Amen.

LOSS OF A BROKEN RELATIONSHIP

The Lord is near to those who are discouraged; he saves those who have lost all hope.

Psalm 34:18

It can be devastating when you lose a relationship. Why is this happening, what did I do, how can I fix this or what did I miss are some of the things that can be said when a person suffers the loss of the broken relationship? Relationships can expire for a variety of reasons such as death, moving away from home, attending college or starting a new beginning. Whatever the reasons are, things are based on information that we know and sometimes we do not. We can come up with a thousand questions as to why this happened and why things worked out the way they did, but just know that there was a reason for the breakup. It may be for the protection of the heart, it may because of illness, it may be because of tragedy, or a host of other reasons, just know you are being protected for a reason and trust God in his plan.

Prayer
Father, I really want to know why? What is it that I was being

protected from, thank you for protecting me when I want to
know your reason? Allow me to take the information and
reasons why in order to be a different and new creature in you.
Amen.

LOSS OF A HOME

*God, you God, will restore everything
you lost; he'll have compassion on you;
he'll come back and pick up the pieces
from all the places where you were
scattered.*

Deuteronomy 30:3

I tried what I could do to try to continue to provide a home for myself and my family. It is hard to fathom that I am not longer in this place that I once thought was my home forever and the blessing that you have entrusted to me. I am now beginning to settle into that this might not have been what was in my best interest and you are shielding me from what is about to come. Lord thank you for this lesson as it is something that I need to learn. I do not see it right [G1]now, but I know that I will need this lesson one, two or even fifteen years from now. I do not understand but I think you for shielding me from something greater.

Prayer

I do not understand how losing my home is best for me, but I know that you have something greater in store for my life. It is hard to accept the initial feelings, but I know that blessings are about to come and fill my life. In Jesus name, Amen.

LOSS OF PREGNANCY

As you do not know the path of the wind, or how the body is formed in a mother's womb, so you cannot understand the work of God, the Maker of all things.

Ecclesiastes 11:5

Lord, I am hurting, and I do not understand why I lost my baby. I prayed and prayed for a child for some many years and I finally got what I prayed for. Then suddenly, my world was rocked to the core as my baby is no longer with me. I am devastated that I was given the precious gift of life and now I cannot continue the journey that I started. I am so angry and do not understand why. I wish I understood why because this is so hard to understand. Lord what are you protecting me from, what information are you hiding from me, what is wrong with my child that I am not able to care for him? Even though I do not understand it must be a reason that you have chosen to shield me from the answers. I am hurting right now and I still do not know why but I am trusting in your will.

Prayer

Father I am so lost, and I do not understand. I really want to know why. I am sorrowful because I have lost my child, but I know you know and control everything in on this earth. I know I won't understand now and will understand it by and by. Amen.

LOSS OF A SIGNIFICANT OTHER

Give thanks in all circumstances; for this is the will of God in Christ Jesus for you.

1 Thessalonians 5:18

Losing a significant can be one of the most devastating things that one has to go through. You never get over it you just learn to live without them. You try to remember the good times, but the bad times resurface as well. Even in the midst of the loss, you still want to know the reasons why. What could I have done to prevent this? Is there anything I could have done? How can I go on? These are the questions and conversations that you have with God about the outcome. Where do I begin to rebuild and how do I even consider love once you are gone? No one will ever replace you or be like you. I wonder if the reasons why will even be provided or explained. I continue to look to God for comfort and often still wonder why.

Prayer

Lord, help me to accept your Will. Help me to understand the reasoning and trust your ways. I acknowledge and give full surrender to you. In your wonderful and magnificent name, Amen.

LOSS OF A BUSINESS

For I know the plans I have for you, declares the Lord, plans for welfare and not for evil, to give you a future and a hope.

Jeremiah 29:11

Lord, you gave me the thought and I have worked toward fulfilling the dream of owning my own business. But there are times when I am not sure what I have got myself into. Somedays things are really hard and other days I can sit back and see the things that I have accomplished. I know that you will continue to direct my path, but it is hard to know that I am losing my business and cannot continue to produce so that the doors can stay open. Help my unbelief and give me a peace of mind. Allow me to recognize that you have something else in store for me. Do I revamp what I had or do I listen for you to give me another idea that will be much better than what I had? Let me open my heart to this new idea and know that you have plans for my future to help me succeed.

Prayer:

A new business will be formed with your help Lord. Allow me to gather all of the ideas and set me aside. Help me to understand what is coming and prepare my heart for more. Amen.

Additional Scriptures on Losses

Psalm 34:17-20

When the righteous cry for help, the Lord hears and delivers them out of all their troubles. The Lord is near to the brokenhearted and saves the crushed in spirit. Many are the afflictions of the righteous, but the Lord delivers him out of them all. He keeps all his bones; not one of them is broken.

2 Corinthians 12:9

But he said to me, "My grace is sufficient for you, for my power is made perfect in weakness." Therefore I will boast all the more gladly of my weaknesses, so that the power of Christ may rest upon me.

Matthew 5:4

Blessed are those who mourn, for they shall be comforted.

Philippians 4:19

And my God will supply every need of yours according to his riches in glory in Christ Jesus.

2 Corinthians 1:3-5

Blessed be the God and Father of our Lord Jesus Christ, the Father of mercies and God of all comfort, who comforts us in all our affliction, so that we may be able to comfort those who are in any affliction, with the comfort with which we ourselves are comforted by God. For as we share abundantly in Christ's sufferings, so through Christ we share abundantly in comfort too.

2 Peter 2:9

Then the Lord knows how to rescue the godly from trials, and to keep the unrighteous under punishment until the day of judgment,

Matthew 5:1-12

Seeing the crowds, he went up on the mountain, and when he sat down, his disciples came to him. And he opened his mouth and taught them, saying: "Blessed are the poor in spirit, for theirs is the kingdom of heaven. "Blessed are those who mourn, for they shall be comforted. "Blessed are the meek, for they shall inherit the earth. ...

Jeremiah 17:10

I the Lord search the heart and test the mind, to give every man according to his ways, according to the fruit of his deeds.

1 Corinthians 6:19-20

Or do you not know that your body is a temple of the Holy Spirit within you, whom you have from God? You are not your own, for you were bought with a price. So glorify God in your body.

John 1:1-51

In the beginning was the Word, and the Word was with God, and the Word was God. He was in the beginning with God. All things were made through him, and without him was not any thing made that was made. In him was life, and the life was the light of men. The light shines in the darkness, and the darkness has not overcome it. ...

Isaiah 40:1-31

Comfort, comfort my people, says your God. Speak tenderly to Jerusalem, and cry to her that her warfare is ended, that her iniquity is pardoned, that she has received from the Lord's hand double for all her sins. A voice cries: "In the wilderness prepare the way of the Lord; make straight in the desert a highway for our God. Every valley shall be lifted up, and every mountain and hill be made low; the uneven ground shall become level, and the rough places a plain. And the glory of the Lord shall be revealed, and all flesh shall see it together, for the mouth of the Lord has spoken..."

REFLECTION ON LOSSES

_____

_____

_____

_____

_____

_____

_____

_____

_____

_____

_____

_____

_____

_____

_____

_____

_____

_____

_____

About the Author

Cherie L. Barnes is a clinician, author, and speaker, child of God and founder of The Healing Group. Cherie is the author of 12 Lessons of Healing Through Grief. As an advocate of healing, Cherie uses her own experiences and others of grief and loss to tell stories that help individuals find meaning in life and support positive actions. Cherie has a Master's degree in Counseling, is a National Certified Counselor, and is a lifelong learner who studies at the University of Life. When she is not glued to her computer, she enjoys cooking, binge-watching the Food Network, writing, and volunteer work. She is currently working on a children's book on grief and loss and a book of poems. For upcoming events and booking visit my website at, www.cheriebarnesauthor.com or join the free Facebook community, The Healing Group, where you will be inspired and find encouragement while healing from grief, loss, and trauma. Visit me at linktr.ee/author_cherieb to connect with me on Facebook, purchase my E-books and to see my latest blog post.